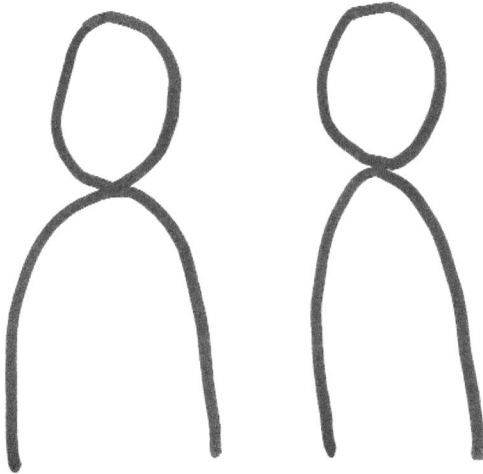

TITLE PAGE

JOCKO

GRAND OAK BOOKS
NEW YORK, NEW YORK
2015

LIBRARY OF CONGRESS CATALOGING-IN-PUBLICATION
DATA : JOCKO SAYS UP YOURS, CONGRESS.

ISBN :   1937727564
          978-1-93772756-7

COVER DESIGN BY JOCKO
PRINTED IN ANTARTICA
    10 9 8 7 6 5 4 3 2 1   BLAST OFF!

HALF-TITLE PAGE

Joe

BLANK PAGE

(INDETERMINATE

PURPOSE)

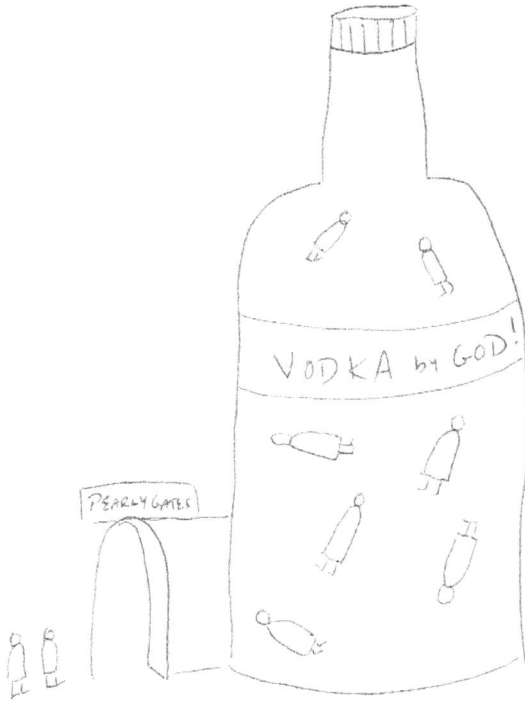

VODKA by GOD!

PEARLY GATES

IRISH HEAVEN

JOCKO

FIZZZZ

HUMAN SKIN
UPHOLSTERY

PEARLY
GATE

FREE

GOLD
TEETH

FREE

HUMAN HAIR

FREE

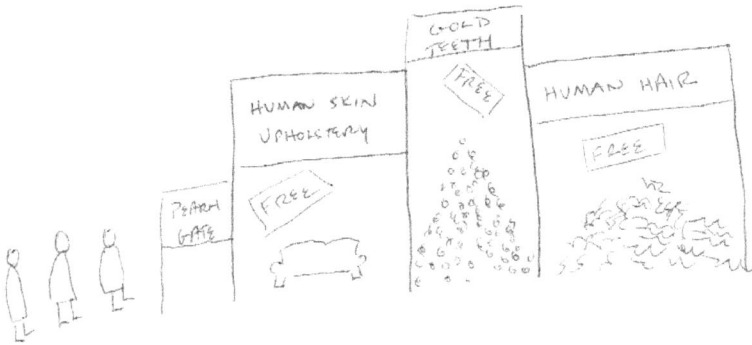

GERMAN HEAVEN

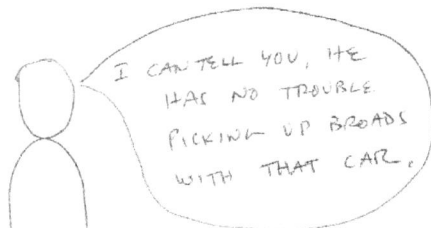

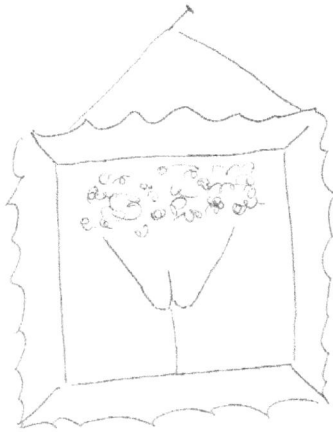

ALSHYMERS CLINIC
ALZHAMERZ
ALSHYMECHERS

OLD FOLKS HOME

© JOCKO

MUSLIM HEAVEN

JOCKO

23

VACANCY

JEWISH HEAVEN

Jocko

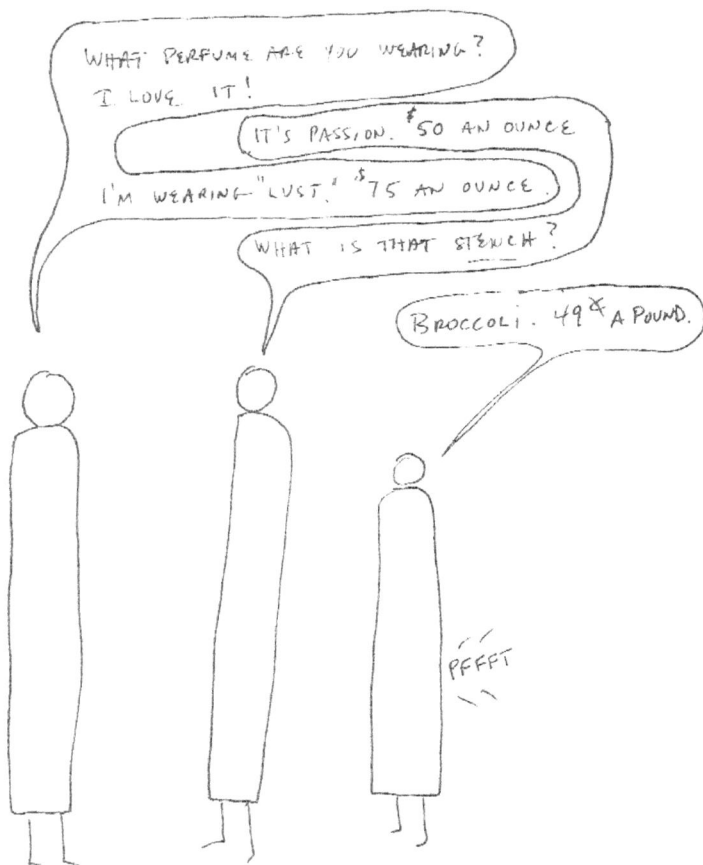

© JOCKO

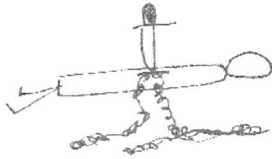

I GUESS YOU WON'T BE. CALLING ME "MR. ROLEY POLEY" ANYMORE.

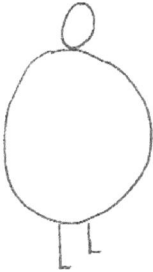

I HOPE HE REMEMBERS TO FEED ME.

WOOF.

JOCKO

GENERAL CUSTER
HERE!

PANTS DOWN AND
BENT OVER!

FREE
FIRE WATER

K-Y
JELLY
HERE

NAKED WHITE WOMEN
WITH
REMOVABLE SCALPS

FREE

WE WAIT LONG
TIME FOR THIS.

NATIVE AMERICAN HEAVEN

Jolke

WOGS
KEEP
OUT

NO IRISH
ALLOWED

RESTAURANT
NO
ENGLISH FOOD

MEET FOREIGN
SOCCER FANS
AND BEAT THE
SHIT OUT OF
THEM
HERE↓

PHOTOS OF
PRINCESS DI'S
VAGINA

FREE

BLOODY
GOOD

BLIMEY!

ENGLISH HEAVEN

Jocko

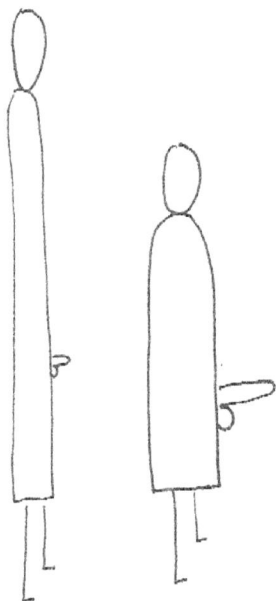

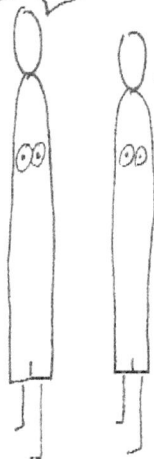

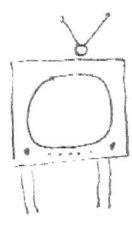

44

SPECIAL OLYMPICS ROCKETTES TRY-OUTS

©JOCKO

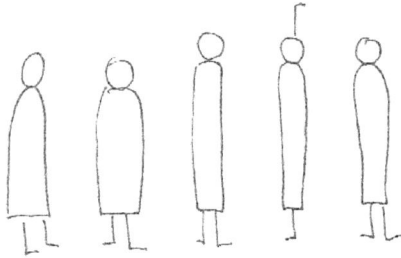

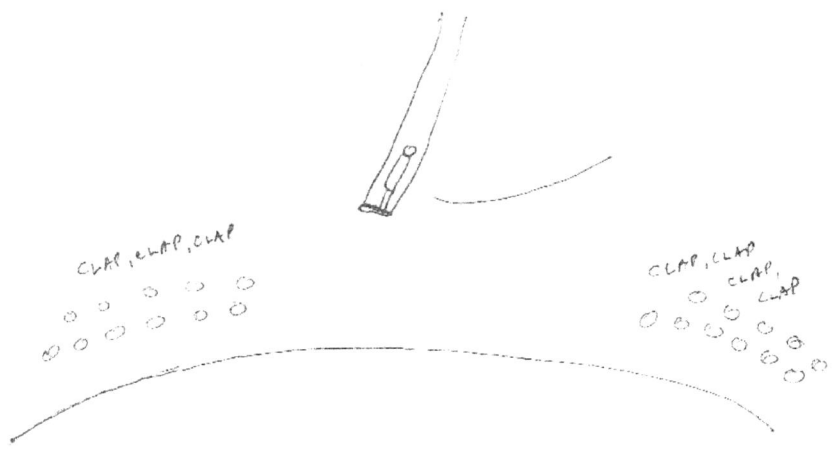

53

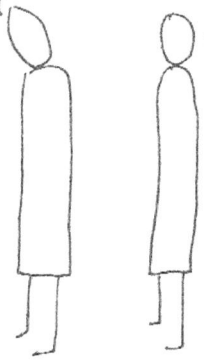

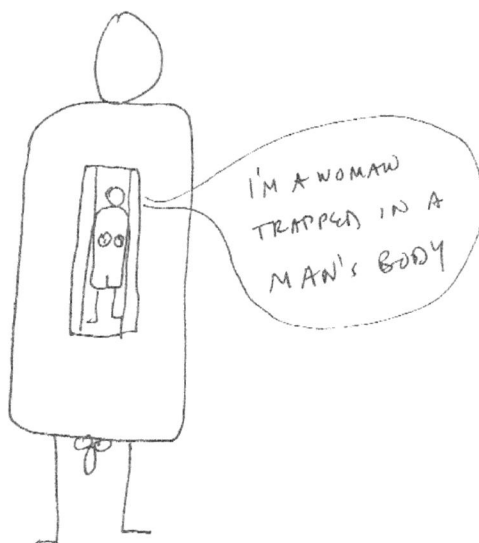

UNFORTUNATELY MR KELLY, THE ONLY DONOR FOR YOUR LIVER TRANSPLANT WAS THIS REALLY BIG FAT SLOB.

© JOCKO

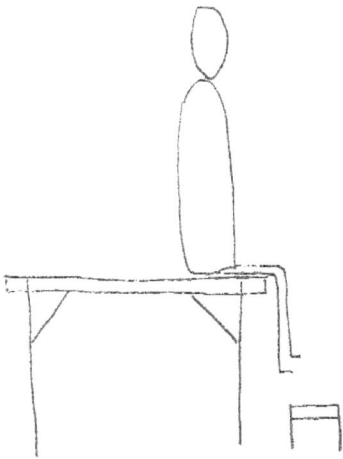

62

71

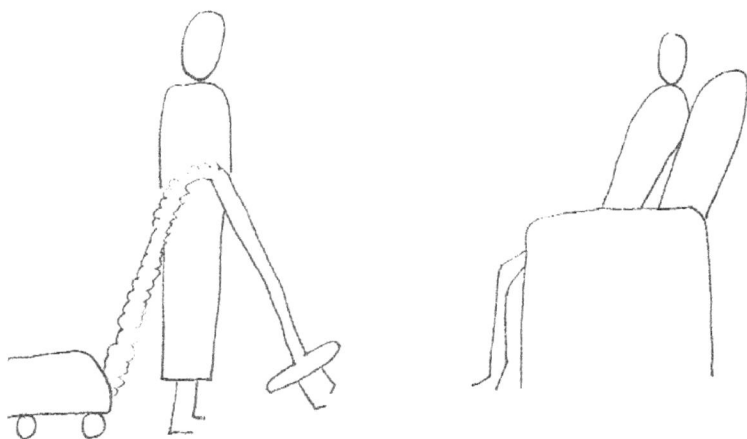

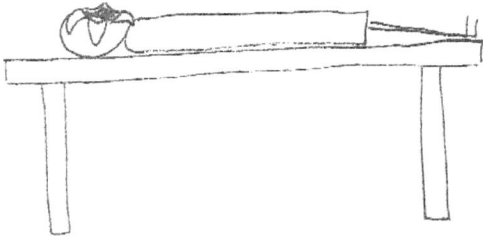

© JOCKO

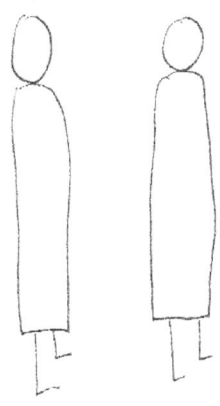

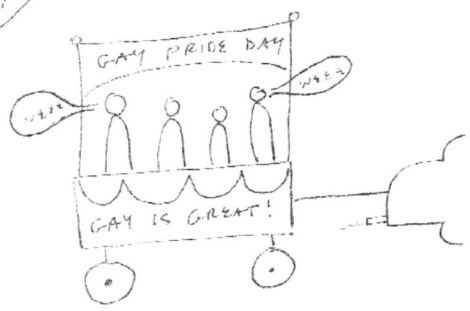

© JOCKO

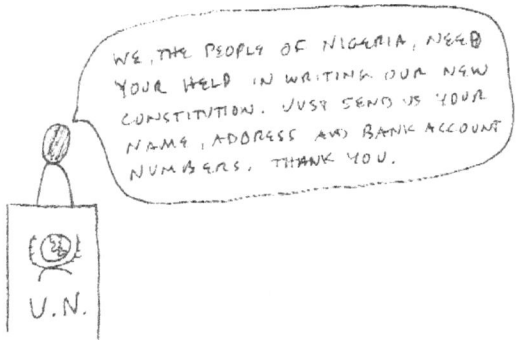
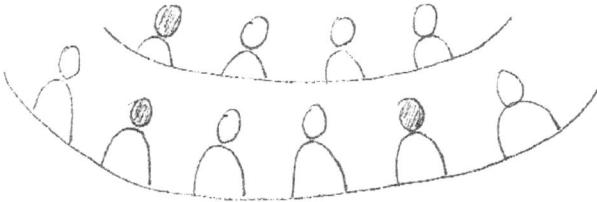

THE WKRAK WEATHER HELICOPTER MADE
FREQUENT VISITS TO THE NUDE BEACH
FOR THE MORBIDLY OBESE.

© Jocko

83

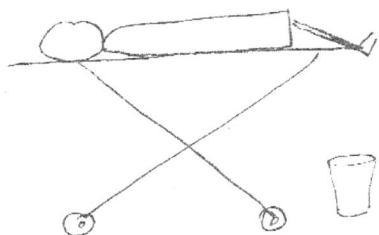

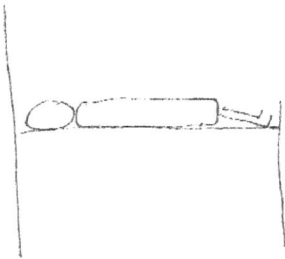

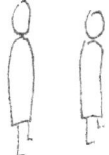

94

GRANNY, YOU & GRAMPS DID A REAL NICE JOB DECORATING THE TREE. VERY ORIGINAL
YEP, WE DID IT THE WAY WE USED TO BACK IN ALABAMA IN THE GOOD OLE DAYS, Y'ALL
© JOCKO

97

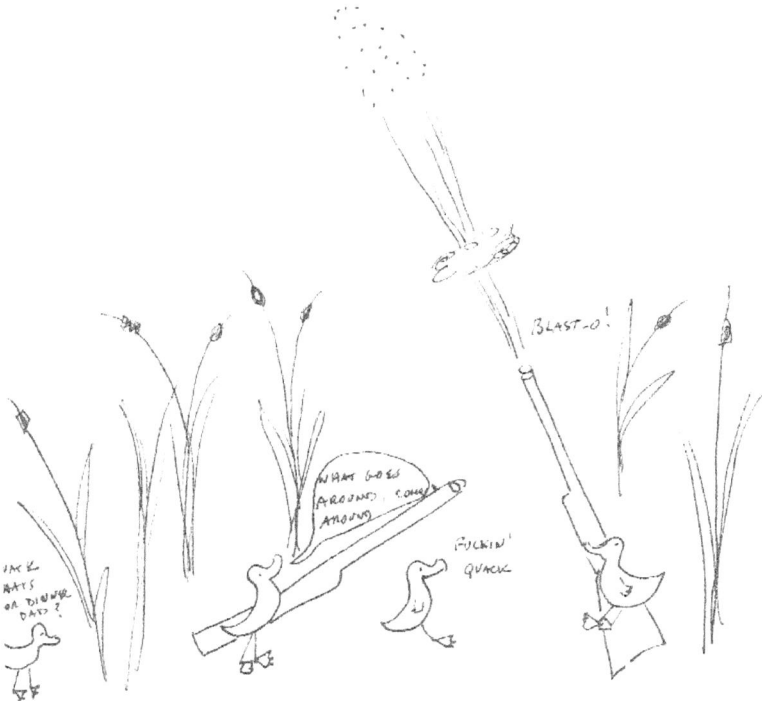

FLAP FLAP

OH SHIT

BLAST-O!

WHAT GOES AROUND, COMES AROUND

FUCKIN' QUACK

JACK RATS OR DINNER RATS?

© JOCKO

© JOCKO

ARIES
SUICIDE
PARLOR

SALE!
DIE HERE
FOR CHEAP!

JACKS
SUICIDE
EMPORIUM

THEY'VE BEEN SPRINGING UP ALL OVER TOWN SINCE THE REPUBLICANS WON THE WHITE HOUSE AGAIN.

© JOULO

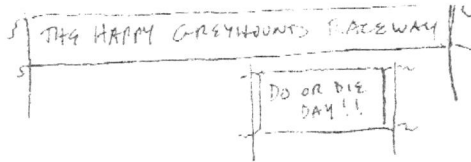

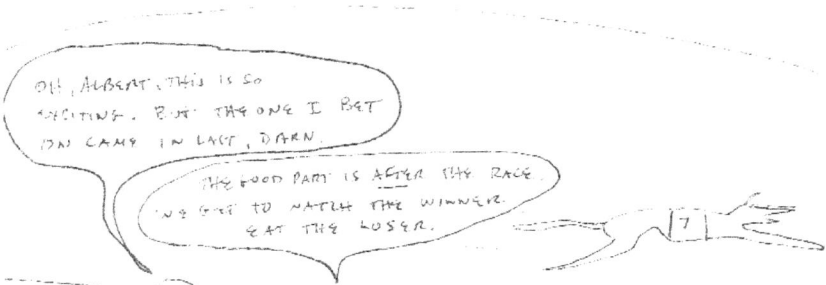

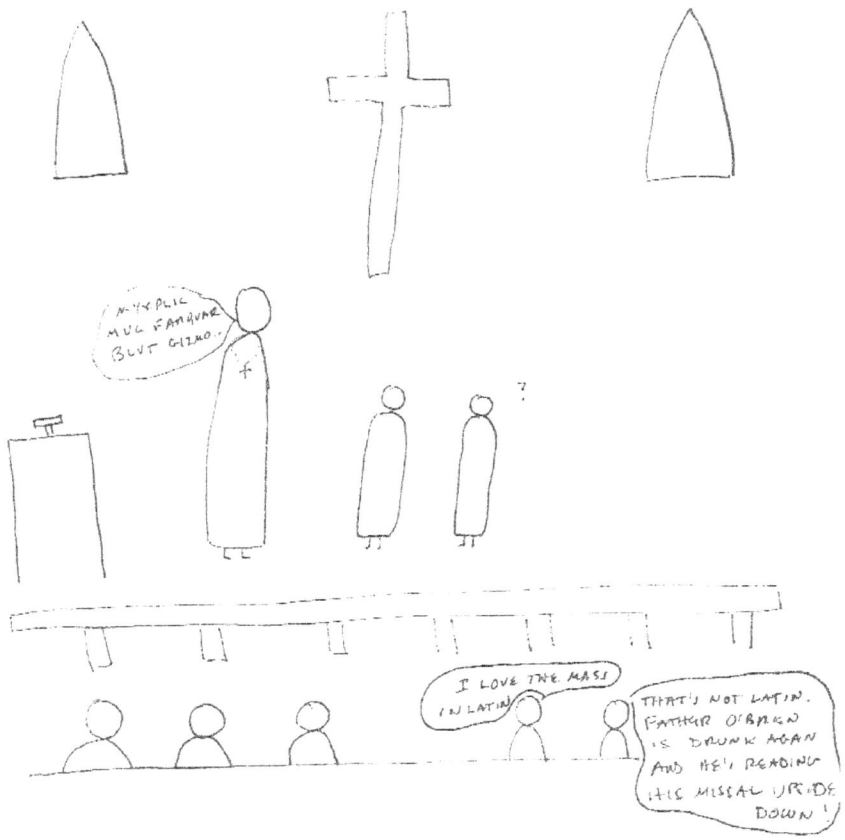

105

108

BLACK HEAVEN

JOCKO

THE
MISS HIROSHIMA CONTEST
1946

FFFT!

CLAP   'LAP   CLAP

JOCKO

112

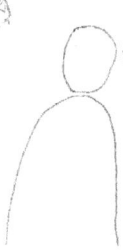

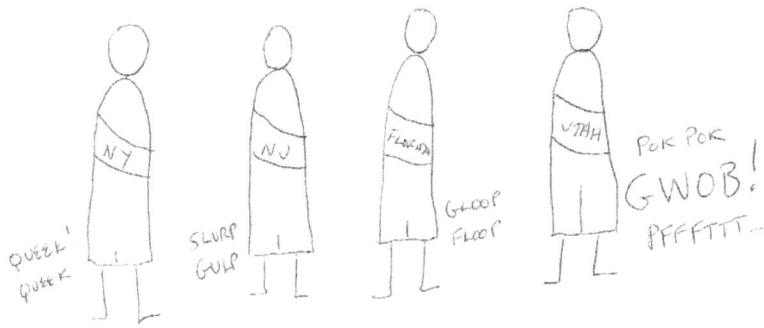

JOCKO

121

AMERICAN
TOBACCO
COMPANY

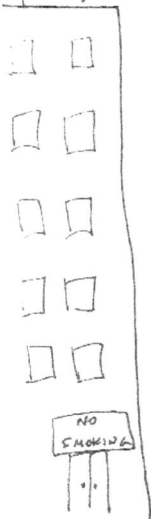

NO
SMOKING

Jocko

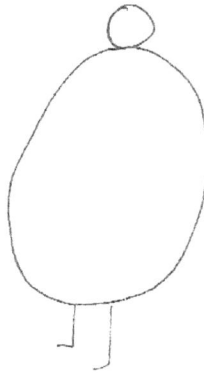

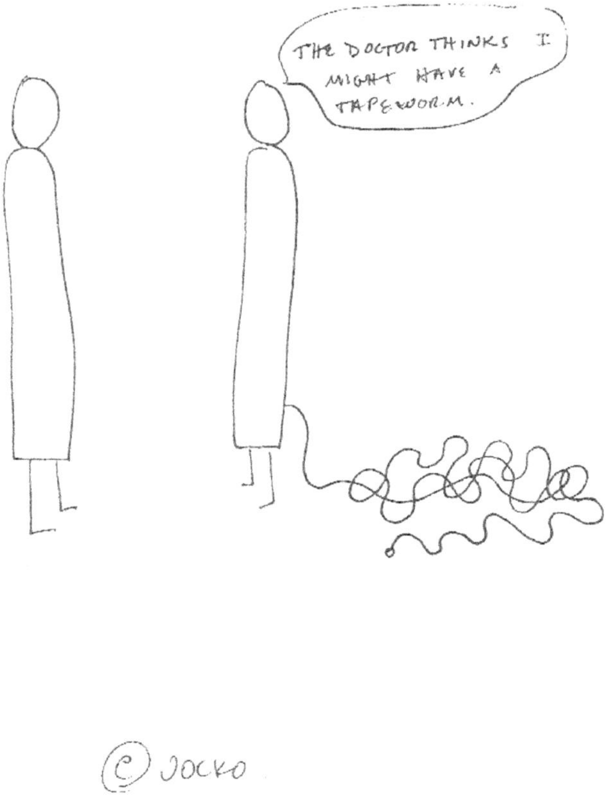
THE DOCTOR THINKS I MIGHT HAVE A TAPEWORM.
© JOCKO

OUR LADY OF PEACE

SERMON SUPPORT THE WAR!

FIRST LUTHERAN CHURCH OF ST. PAUL

WORD THE JEWS REALLY DID KILL JESUS

FIRST BAPTIST CHURCH

TODAY IT IS RIGHT TO KILL ABORTION DOCTORS

YOU CAN ALWAYS TELL THE MORAL CHARACTER OF A NATION BY ITS RELIGIOUS VALUES.

© JOCKO

139

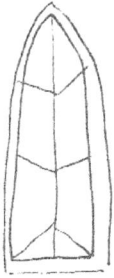

144

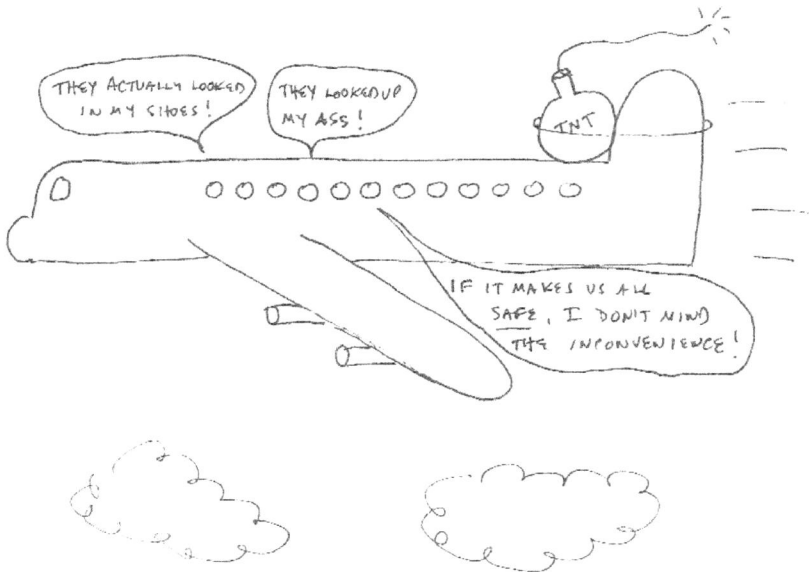

145

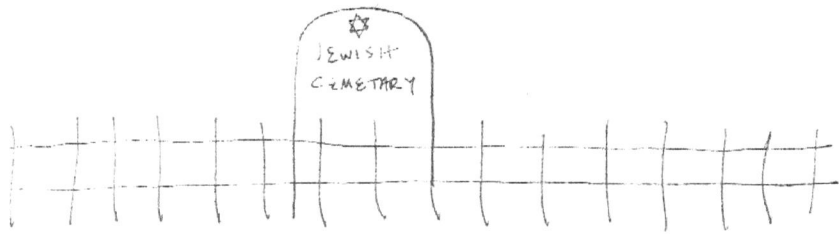

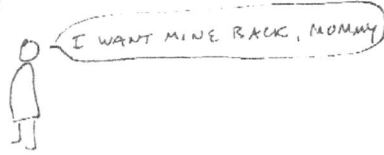

148

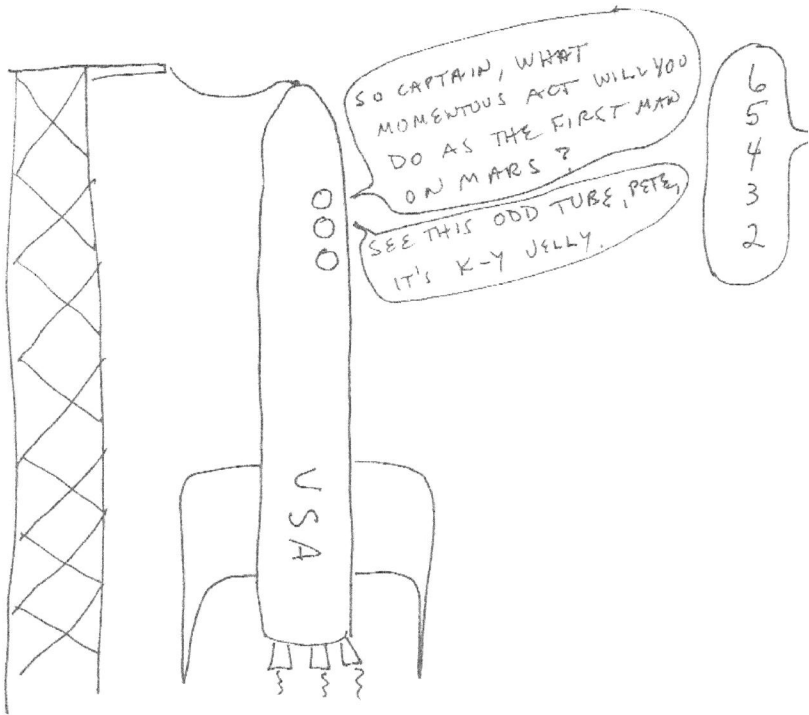

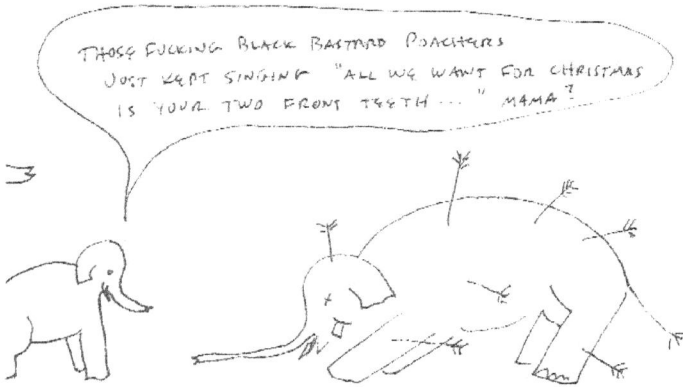

155

158

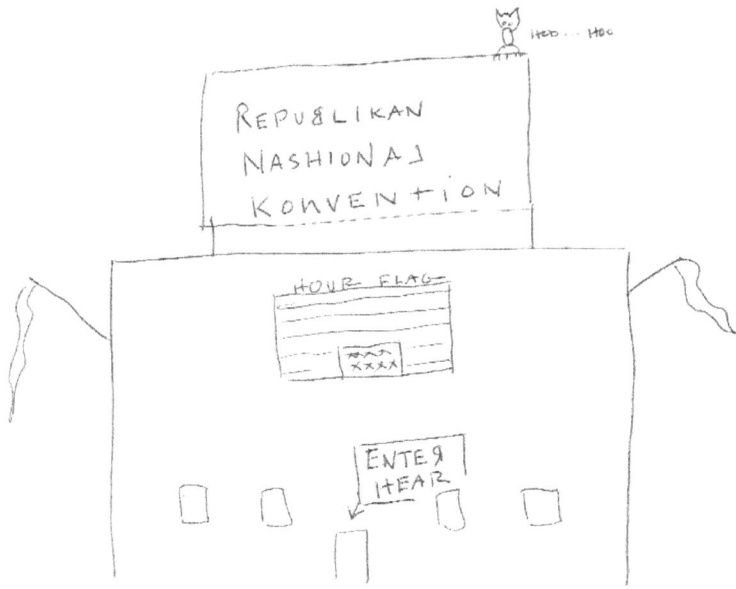

167

169

172

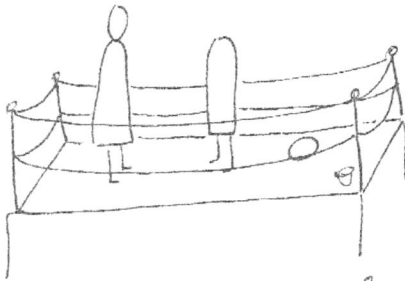

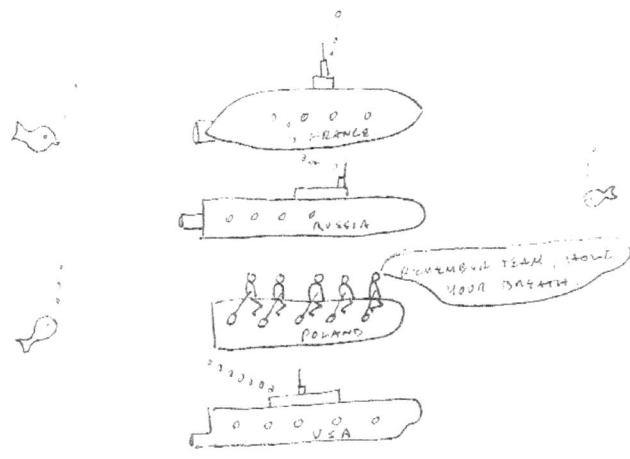

FIRST OLYMPIC
SUBMARINE
RACE

FRANCE

RUSSIA

REMEMBER TEAM, HOLD
YOUR BREATH

POLAND

USA

© JOCKO

181

I THINK THAT PLOW DRIVER JUST CLEARED THE PLAYGROUND INSTEAD OF THE PARKING LOT.

© JOCKO

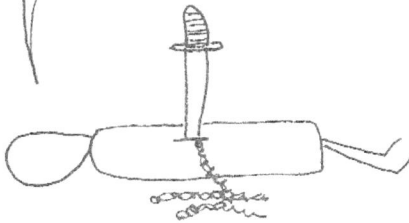

185

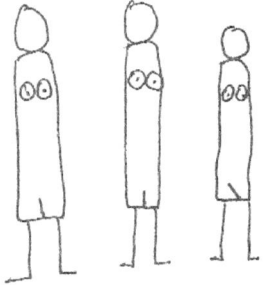
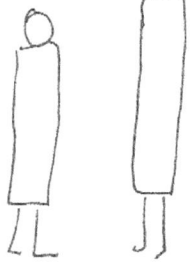

© Jocke

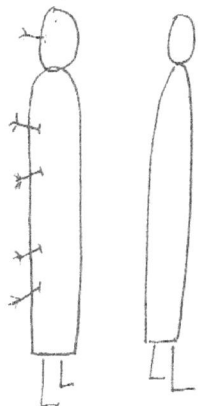

194

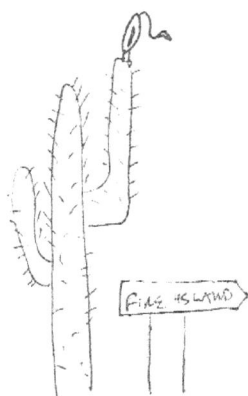

200

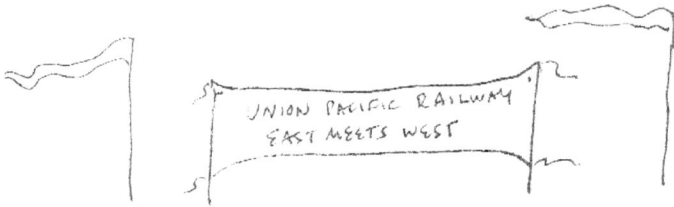
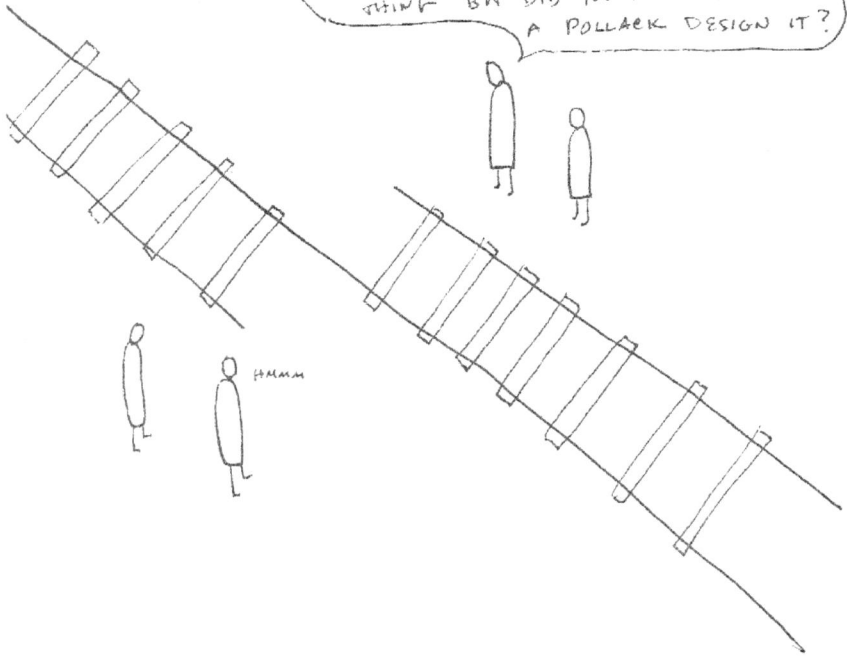

© JOCKO

203

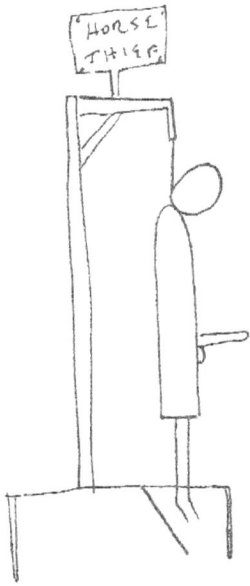

204

MOMMY, THE TOOTH FAIRY CAME INTO MY ROOM LAST NIGHT. HE LET ME TOUCH HIS MAGIC WAND AND THEN WE WRESTLED A BIT, HE GROANED AND THEN LEFT A QUARTER UNDER MY PILLOW.
THAT WAS NO TOOTH FAIRY. IT WAS YOUR FUCKING UNCLE LESTER!
© JOCKO

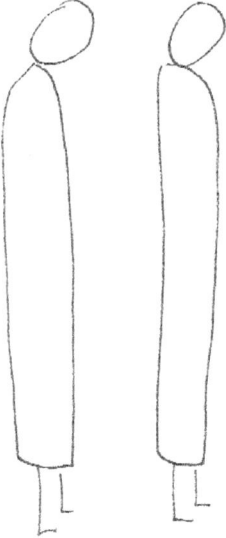

© JOCKO

© JOCKO

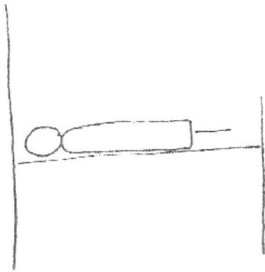

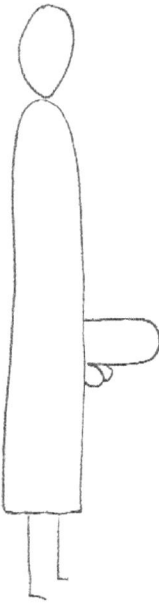

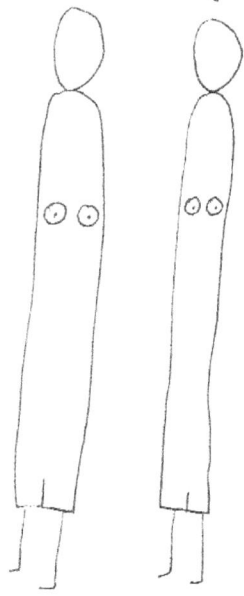

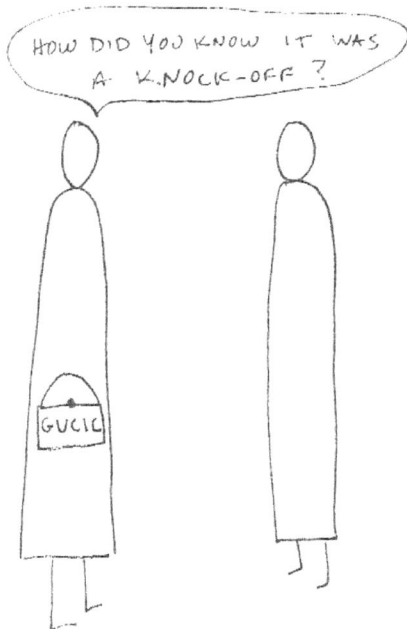

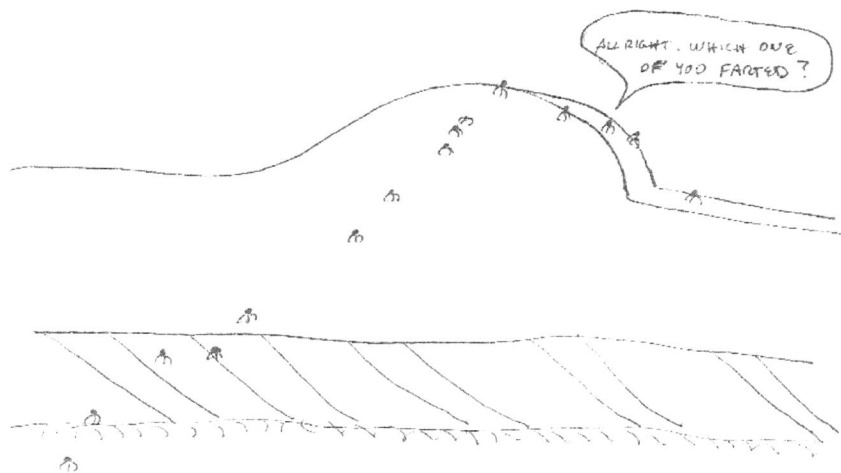

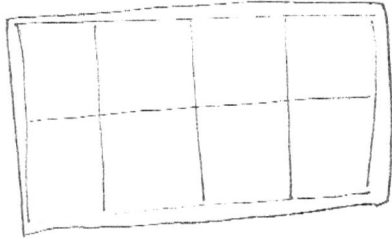

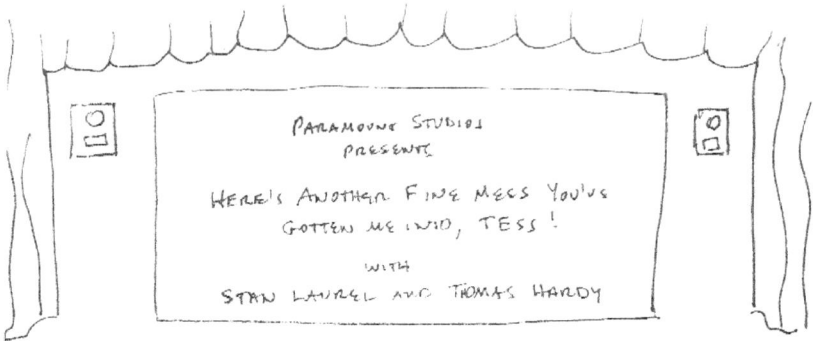

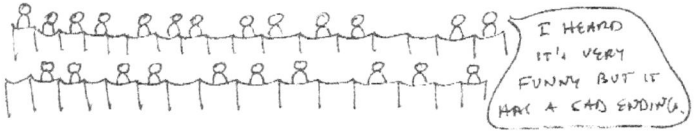

224

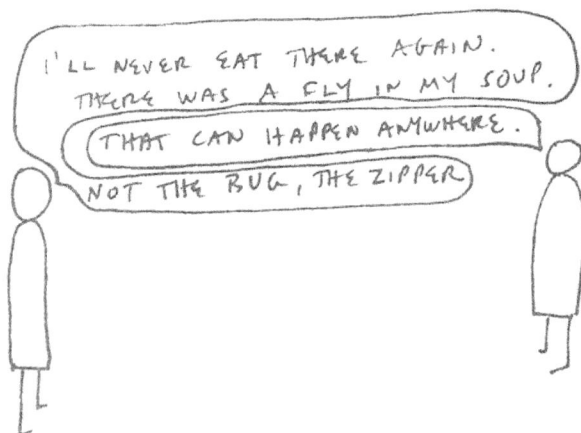

227

228

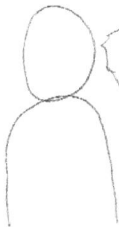

233

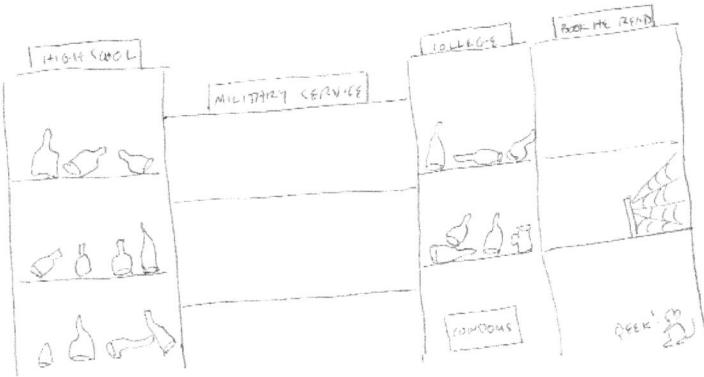

GUCCI · PUCCI · ITOOCHI · COCCHI

THE POLISH GOVERNMENT DONATED THIS YEAR'S TREE

ROCKEFELLER CENTER

JOCKO

236

www.ingramcontent.com/pod-product-compliance
Lightning Source LLC
LaVergne TN
LVHW051228080426
835513LV00016B/1478